GRIME KERBSTONE

PSALMS

MIGGY ANGEL

Published by Celandor Books
3 Lawn Mill Road,
Kimberley,
Nottingham.
NG16 2HD

Email: info@celandor.co.uk

All rights reserved. This book is copyrighted and must not be copied, reproduced, transferred, distributed, leased, licensed or publicly performed in any way except as permitted in writing by the publishers.

No part of this book may be reproduced or stored in an information retrieval system (other than for purposes of review) without the express permission of the publisher in writing.

© 2013 Miggy Angel

First published in 2013.

ISBN 978-1-908484-02-4

A Climbing Mountains imprint for Celandor Books
www.celandor.co.uk

Cover illustration is from an original work by the artist Trish Evans. © 2012 Trish Evans.
www.road-works.org.uk

The Wind was first published by *Kill Author* magazine

Beholden was first published by *3:AM* magazine

For me mum

(Sheila Ann James)

Contents

PART ONE: TO THE MANOR BORN

The Stairwell Dahlia
The Painter
The Scholar
The World's Tallest Man
Under The Knife
The Funeral
Blood Rites
Heritage
Murder On The Block
Flower In The City

PART TWO: GENTRIFIED TIMES

The Plantation
The Street Beneath
The Riot
The Graduation
Beholden
Another Urban Myth
Walk, Don't Walk
The Bog
The Wind
This Neighbourhood Has Been Regenerated
Gentrified Times

PART THREE: THE CRACK THRU WHICH HE CREPT

The Story Of Crack

Something Happened On The Way To The Crack House

I Am God's Trusted Pharmacist

Anointment

Sing Me A Song

The Prophet

Mother Mercy

The Phoenix

The Lament

PART FOUR: ASPHALT RUNWAYS

The Bookworm

Notes To A Young Mystic

I Am The Riot You Seek

Songs Sung In The First Register

Narrow Alleys

The Linguist

The Bell

Scallywag Standing On The Balcony Of Tate Modern

♦

Acknowledgments & Thanks

Foreword

When a person loses authorship of their life's narrative, as I did at a young age, any activity which provides an opportunity to wield the conductor's stick & marshal the orchestra becomes incredibly attractive. Writing is such an activity. As the poet Charles Wright has said, "Poetry is an exile's art. Anyone who writes it seriously is writing from an exile's point of view." Writing is survival. Writing is sticking a flag in the terrain of your life & making a claim on the territory. Writing is confirmation, a telegram from you to yourself, telling you that you're still alive. Writing is the last outpost of vital, independent thought in lobotomized times. Writing is a proactive act in a prescribed world. Writing is a connection to our innate wellspring of creativity, which is our connection to the magical box of tricks which is the universe. Imagination is the umbilical chord connecting us to god – creating is the closest we get to being gods ourselves.

My first attempts at writing were whilst just out of addiction rehab, living in a halfway house off Ladbroke Grove in London in my early twenties - & followed me into a homeless-person's unit in Earl's Court. I recall that these initial lunges at literature were incredibly painful. Having read no books I had no reference points other than my own energies & impulses. Which sounds potentially liberating: but as my primary animator was an incendiary vein of anger & resentment, my writing was consequently mostly rabid doggerel & personal vitriol against humanity.

I felt in those days unbelievably low. It's hard now to convey the sense I had of myself as worthless. Every day was akin to walking barefoot on hot coals.

Why did I persist with writing thru the long days & nights when I produced nothing of note - neither a glimpse of potential success or future promise? I do not know. Maybe it's because writing was all I had, the only door still left ajar. I was beset by a furious ambition, a wild, energised desire to write, & write better.

Writing really began for me in reading. I have been mentored by a procession of men & women (writers), some dead, others whom I'll probably never meet. All of whom gifted me a tacit permission to write & unwittingly educated me in the arcane & blessed art of abidance, & reception. What a life these touch-stone persons have bestowed upon this scallywag committed to a life of attuning his sensibilities & forging a receptacle from his heart.

I offer to you my first book of poems. I hope you receive it as an invitation to go & write your own.

Miggy Angel – Nottingham, 2012

There are not nine million stories in the city.
There is one story
with nine million endings
& nine million ways to begin.

GRIME KERBSTONE PSALMS

(Litany For The) Street

Street, rattle your skulls, shake

your pouch of owl's claws, baste

my charred heart in your asphalt kiln,

street, spit the steel bit from your mouth,

bare your kerbstone gait, grin

the imp of your orifice, street, chipped

chieftain, roar round corners, lift

your skirt, snap your garter's width,

street, teach me girth, distance

in thickets thick with barbs, will

my dirge to worm its blind reach, street,

shorn my sins, singe my effluence,

sing my floral chorus, street, dunce

my hat, denounce my genius, ascend

my tongue's conventions, assign your diesel

assonance, dissemble my dissident

heart, street, sleep awake, relieve

your canals in my offal, sift your surplus

of alphabet soup, street, iron your religions,

surrender your soothsayers, embalm

your erogenous boroughs, harm

your hordes, hinder your harbours, marshal

your wards, armour your ardour, street,

twelve parts ghost, shark your vast ruts,

fin your carved currents, bollock

your relics, street, pop your chops, flop

your fat's roll, lure your victims, suckle

your rodents, nipple your vermin

kin, teat your spawn omens, spurn

your spurs, spar your paws, street,

teem your vagrants, wish your wants,

will your worst, but street please,

please, spare me my dreams.

PART ONE:

TO THE MANOR BORN

". . . to the delight of the poetic gutter boys in the little grey streets."

G.K. Chesterton

The Stairwell Dahlia

The cliché goes that there ain't
nothing grows in a tower-block stairwell

but needles & rat mess, urine
aromas & trash, urban detritus,

soiled nappy-bombs, crushed
crack-pipe cola cans & spunked condoms.

The ever-expanding patch-quilt hurts
of feral council-estate children.

The stairwell's where we whiled away our days,
especially remember those wet

bank holiday Mondays, hazed
thru clouds of weed smoke. & what

day doesn't have its green shoots
as well as its black deficits? Yes

the stairwell saw violence. Fat
lips split on the kiss of gnarled

knuckles, red-eyed heads rolled,
unanimous, generous knockouts, & theft.

Flat-footed policemen chasing too-fast juveniles
in Reeboks across the asphalt roofs of flats,

drug deals curdled sour in the pale
of betrayal. Scores settled in claret

rosettes spilled upon concrete steps
& once, a rape. But, you sit anywhere

long enough, bound to see the spectrum's
full rotation. On these steps I seen

bonds born between sons of broken
homes, & waif girls learn to wife

the woman inside them. I seen moonlight lend the mise-en-scene a divine

countenance. Where shadows, transcendent,
become king & queen for the night. I seen

hope incubate its seed in the mouth
of a gold-toothed smile. Once,

on floor thirteen, where the angle
of the gutter cuts across the stairwell

with love's X, I saw one tall white flower,
a dahlia, growing from a drain. I swear.

The Painter

Standing in line at the bank you notice a childhood friend enter & stand in line behind you. You stare straight ahead, as if at something more important. You do not turn around & acknowledge the man, who you have not seen for some years, as to do so would mean comprehending his fully receded hairline, admitting your lost years & the fact that you are visiting the bank holding a loaded revolver in your jacket pocket. If you just continue to look straight ahead you are all forever angels preserved in the formaldehyde of your yearning. Young kids with brick-dust faces & the requisite cheeky, delinquent grins. You recall how an old man had once walked past you & your friends as you hugged the street corner & there was an altercation. Before the old man was killed by one cleanly dispatched punch to the temple he had asked you what you wanted to be when you grow up & you had told him, "I wanna paint pictures."

The Scholar

Ten years old & already I know
where the souls of this city are buried.
Ten years old & already I have discerned
how those weeds which worm up

thru the cracks are the speech-bubbles of ghosts,
dormant beneath my kerbstone-hounding
feet. Ten years old & already I know
that the barbed-wire wound about

the facades of my locale are the unspooled
steel terrors of my barbed mind. Ten
years old & already I know how the dark
clouds above my block speak my history: adrift,

migrating west, anchorless, bruised
by the rain they hold. Ten years old
& already my school satchel stores a ton
of skulls, picked clean of their skin

by the lean years of Aquarius. Pink brains
membranes & dreams evaporate into mist

at the behest of these streets' obsidian magic.
Ten years old & already my emerald eyes confess

a lust for violence, the scolding of sentience,
the extinguishing of suns. In geography class
I tell my teacher that I am a genius of the terrain,
that my map exceeds the territory. In English

I astonish the class with my exquisite, linguistic
science: when I say the word Gun & mean it
the sky turns black. In mathematics you best
stand back, as my arithmetic hurts. My favourite

summation, being: 1 son + the pistol's anointing
= 1 numb human tomb, a weeping woman,
widowed & un-tethered from motherhood. Now,
teacher, I dare you to put me on detention.

The World's Tallest Man

My father is dead to me now. I climb my father's frame & I stand on my father's shoulders. We put on a long brown Macintosh coat which covers us both. Only my head is visible from the top & down beneath protrude my father's legs. His arms fill the sleeves of the coat & both his hands are gloved. My father & I, posing as the world's tallest man, walk out into the street. We walk for some time thru the city, my father stopping every now & then to reminisce beside landmarks which resonate with him but which I do not recognise. "This is where I met your mother," he says. I watch a dog piss upon a lamppost. My father reaches into the pocket of the Macintosh & produces a pack of cigarettes & a lighter. He stretches up & places a cigarette in my mouth, then lights it. "How many times I got to tell you, dad," I say. "I don't smoke yet." "Be quiet," he says, "& blow a smoke ring at the sun for your father. The world's tallest man."

Under The Knife

The blade that bleeds the cheek
of its impish innocence, & wipes
the smile from crooked juveniles
forever, is the blade I deigned to dodge

my whole life. My mother, said
"Don't go getting your face cut, like
them idiots outside. Your skin's Keloid,
doesn't scar like those other boys

round here. Your scars don't heal proper.
Just like your father." So, the night
my friend, Charlie, returns from A&E
with red knots of ragged stitches

holding the split halves of his face
together in their solace &
begs us not to make him laugh
because he can't grin against

the bows of plastic thread pulled tight
thru his cheek & lips, as we tickle

his heart thru the terrain of his bruised

ribcage, I have an overwhelming urge

to open Charlie's face with my hands

like a book, & take a long hard look

at just what it is us cobble-stone kids

are hiding inside us.

The Funeral

Whilst walking thru the city you discover a 'you' shaped hole in the ground. Right at that moment you experience a 'de-ja-vu' feeling of having been here before. So you know that you're about to climb down into the 'you' shaped hole even before you do it. You lay on your back, your arms stretched out by your sides in a crucified pose, torso & limb proportions moulded perfectly to the hole's cast. Now you're looking up at the night sky, remembering the night you fell down to Earth from the constellation during a comet shower. Your arrival here leaving this 'you' shaped hole in the ground. As you lay in the 'you' shaped hole everyone you've ever known begins to fill the hole with shovels full of ash. Now you are a seed. Somebody clicks their fingers & it begins to rain. Your flower will be the tallest in the city. By day, children shall play upon the stem. At night, by popular demand, a gallows.

Blood Rites

I do not remember the girl's name, who
lived in the flats above the swings.

What I recall is how she would descend
the stairwell like an apparition, a premonition

of something not masculine & more dangerous
for it. She would laugh at her own jokes, ask

the boys whether our balls had dropped yet, or
how often we tossed off. I was no more than ten

& this girl, older than us all in supple flesh &
defiant soul, would wait until I sat upon the swing

to begin her initiation. She straddled my lap, faced
my front & ground her pelvis on my cock.

"Say what you like," she'd say, "but don't tell me
it ain't hard." I blushed, tempered the flood, her

hot breath paralysed me with want. When the girl
began to date we watched the older men arrive in cars

with stallion-power engines, electric windows,
speakers built for stadiums & leather seats

apt for fucking on. She continued to sit in our laps
& swing, but not one of us kopped so much as a kiss.

She had a little brother who wore a parka, whatever
the weather. One night during hot rain, we caught him

on his own & half killed him. In violence we exorcised
the sex we never got to expend on his sister.

Heritage

I remember as schoolchildren
being taken by the institution
to an exhibition of some such
collected, arranged pomp & nonsense
(peculiarly British).

I recall us so small, multi coloured,
of multi ethnicity, scallywags & ragamuffins
from the inner-city
being expected to embrace
what we were presented with
as our history, our inheritance
our worth - but being aware of its irrelevance.

We children were not interested
in the exhibits. Instead
were lost in play & ecstatic
at the miraculous effects of dragging the soles
of our shoes on the garish shag carpet
then touching each other, or the copper banisters.

Sparks of static electric flew
from our hands, bugs of light
exploding on our finger ends.

We were conductors of lightning.
Neither British, English
fish nor fowl, but cousins
to thunder, kin
to the cosmos,
with bright futures
behind us.

Murder On The Block

Once the local reporters' copy is compiled,
their plastic interest fast receded to the collation
of cold facts; once the vigil of rubbernecks
from adjoining blocks moves on, their hungering
for macabre portraits sated; once the forensic
pathologists in jump-suits have carefully raped
the space for evidence; once the cordon tape
is cut like a child's umbilical chord, or the grand
opening of a department store by a mediocre
media-star; once the crime scene is let rest, like
an undressed wound yawning its numb hymn,
a wide red hole burned in the locale; once
the mother has lit the candle she shall never blow out
& knelt in desolation in the eternal shrine
of her grieving mind; once the father has recalled
the flight from Lagos, remembered the dream
he had of Abraham - required by god to sacrifice
a son, Isaac, the penance of an immigrant, & how
he awoke to hold the boy's hand tightly, like
a promise, till the plane landed & the family walked
into a bleached world of asphalt, scraps, & malice;
once the corner youths return to play on the spot

where the city street turned molten & swallowed
another morsel of innocence; once the boys begin
again to chat their shit & bounce their ball; once
the tenner-rock shotters on bmx bikes return
to the crack-spot he died upon, to disseminate
their white & brown fractions of heaven; the one
solace - how moonlight & faint bloodstain
provide the prism, the mirror's echo, which reflects
the murdered boy's red cells up thru a column
of light, back to his celestial source in the cosmos.

Flower In The City

This is how you plant a flower in the city. I take one barbed fist, wield it with ballistic force, follow thunder's white course down thru the electric column which sombre light-bolts & raindrops traverse. With the unclipped force of a lightning fork I punch straight into the world. Rip the ground's abdomen open. Push five rheumatoid, man-mongrel fingers right into the guts of this hushed, corporeal animal. The street pulsates, tenement tendons flex, the locale undulates, windows break into choruses of glass shards, domicile walls fail, roofs unmoor, the hovel is humbled. Plyboard homes gutted like wild boars, spilling their offal, cargo their innards. In the hole my jack-hammer hand nails into this organ crevice of the planet's severed girth, I spit the seed of a broken tooth, fill with a mother's dawn-dusted promises & wait for my flower to grow thru the deficit.

PART TWO:

GENTRIFIED TIMES

"In murky corners of old cities
where everything – horror, too –
is magical."

Charles Baudelaire

The Plantation

Welcome to the plantation, where we work the fields of dreams. We pluck them out at their roots, unscrew them bulb by bulb from the soil of collective unconscious. Once disconnected we collect them in the baskets of our forgetting. Did you see the lights go out? First those of our mothers & fathers, then those of our sons & daughters. Once those, what do we care of our own, or those of our neighbours? We toil for the master of many broken promises. Our bent backs echoing with the diamonds of our labours: our perspiration. Tattooed beneath the rays, we are depressed & mutilated in his gaze.

Welcome to the plantation. We work eagerly & willingly!

It is a known fact that the sun beats sweetly harsher after the black crow, black as the black heart, has flown beneath it.

I am winking as I say this.

The Street Beneath

Down on the street beneath
the broken window on the 3rd floor
of a consecrated tenement block
a puddle of glass shards shimmered
like a river's amorphous surface.

Another neighbourhood dispute,
one more brick delivered into orbit
for a failed drug debt.

I stood above the pond of glass
& peered down into it.
Thru the shattered quartz
like a microscope
& the squint of a stitch-browed lunatic
the street beneath was magnified.

Bequeathed to me a vision
of fly ash, slag cement, aggregate,
gravel limestone, granite. & further
I saw beneath the Earth's crust, witnessed
micro-organisms rapt in apocalyptic raptures,

the turning overtures of forces willing themselves
into existence. Intuited seismic waves
irritating the seismograph. The vibrating drum
of a field of magnetism, a culture of gas
& hot air - molecules, atoms, ions, electrons,
the perpetual street falling thru itself.

Carrying the neighbourhood into an eternity
of broken windows,
graffitied phoneboxes,
militant militants,
disenfranchised franchises,
& children holding hands.

Walking forever after shelter
into the hot hollow of the planet.

The Riot

When the government
announced the cuts
I stopped eating.

My body grew
a waxy cloak.

I stood upright.
Stood naked,
stood white, like
a candlestick.

I torched the wick
of my hair
& burned.

Around this flame
parched moths
with a singular purpose
shall conflagrate.

The Graduation

The citizens are happy. News of our success has reached us. We gather upon the avenues & boulevards, we horde the sidewalks. The city children appear & begin to dress us in long black gowns. We look up, as that is where the external view is watching us from & we stare straight down the lens. As one organ we remove our hats – for we are wearing hats! - & we throw our hats into the air. The hats fly into the sky, pirouette, then rain down upon us. All except for mine. My hat continues its ascent, it climbs the vaporous stairs. I watch it rise up past the clouds into orbit, heading for the Milky Way. I know that the reason my hat does not fall to the ground like the others is because only frauds float. As my hat becomes cosmic, somewhere an astronomer with a propensity for prophecy watches my hat thru a telescope & says, "It is nigh." I hear thunder in the South.

Beholden

I see Zeus
waiting in the checkout
queue. Fallen
on hard times, yet
still magnificent.
His striking, aquiline
profile, that white mane
a staircase to heaven.

Stuffing sausage-rolls
in his pockets,
his eyes fixed, shiftily
on the shelves
of Greek yoghurt.

Another Urban Myth

The man with the tan, tawny owl tattoo
on his arm. Short-sleeve shirt

embalms chest, exposes limbs.
The bird, perched on the branch

of the bicep, its eyes like wells,
watchful as the water they would hold,

see straight along crooked streets,
winged black witch of the concrete forest.

This tattoo art not prison fodder,
no Giro-cheque nor Biro-pen branded this man

with this bird. Less art, more
spectral birthmark. I knew this man

with the owl tattoo. Knew him enough
to nod at him & for him to nod back.

I know how an armada of dealers
have surrendered their wares to his cold

barrel-eyes, his shotgun
promises. I knew him as the abandoned

care-baby, orphaned nuisance. Grew
pumped on the gas of neglect, chomped

the bit of resentment. Man of no kin,
man of no clan, island of one.

On the night they came for him,
stitched the hole in his axis with a single

projectile, no owl was present upon him.
The bird who had kept watch upon

the cherub, like all great urban myths,
left no witnesses & vanished.

Walk, Don't Walk

Those two figures who live inside the lightbox at the pedestrian crossing. The green man - a symbol of progress. See his arm out straight, his leg extended into the future. Glorious future! Which he bids us to walk into with confidence. But wait. The red man appears. Stock still, his arms by his side. A sentry of caution. Stop & think, he says, Imagine where each step leads us. The future is uncertain. We move towards oncoming machinations, dark loomings await us. We heed his ominous divinations.

As the city sleeps & nobody patrols the streets, those twilit hours when the metropolis mislays its purpose - the green man & the red man, what of them then? Do they put aside their differences? Does the green man climb up into the red man's domain? Do they observe common courtesies, are beverages shared, biscuits? Does the one see his reflection in the other? Do they realise how they symbolise the erroneous dualism at the heart of our understanding? Are they Apollo & Dionysus, the lightbox they reside in, the Island of Delos?

The Bog

In the cryptic public toilet
dank & dark
as an alligator's mouth
you stand
holding a struck match
in one hand.

Your inheritance
in the other.

Urinating
while reading the walls.
They say:

Tracy loves Helen,

Nottingham Forest
are batty men,

your mama
is so fat
she makes obesity
look anorexic,

the world shall end
on your birthday,

Scorpios
are saints with pincers,

call this number
for the healing
of your troubled soul.

The flame shall singe
your fingers, &
your silent pause
before the burn
a reverence
for a hell of men's urinals, &
the gospels
of the city's gutter prophets.

The Wind

In the final assessment we all choose a single action & repeat it into infinity. That man there cannot stop adjusting his rear-view mirror, this one here is playing with his cufflinks. There's a woman who walks the city banging people's bins with a long stick. My mother would wind an electric eel around her middle finger as her eyes burned sulphur. My father walked the block's circumference in an anti-clockwise stoop. There are those whose actions mimic an eclectic range but really are invariable. I keep getting back up. The tallest building in the city retreats back into the earth a millimetre each year. There's this one bullet that haunts the metropolis in search of a recipient it shall never meet. The farmhand counts his sheep diligently but is always one sheep down when he returns from the valley. I keep on getting back up. The wind keeps on whispering, "Stay down."

This Neighbourhood Has Been Regenerated

The city streets
were a barren dead-end
of shop-fronts with their lights on,
advertisements, a mass

of enticing enticements.
We pavement tramps were weighed down,
pressed upon by the top hats & tails
we were wearing.

All dressed up & nowhere to go!
We stood barefoot on our tip-toes
peering thru the waxed windows
of the restaurant. In the glass

we saw the reflections
of our own unshaven faces,
big grey beards as old as the Millennia.
Inside was a reception

of like-minds & make-weights,
big-shots & long-&-shorts, dining
a la carte. They ate fried brains,
sautéed bollocks, stewed fingers,

organ kebabs, skewered eyeballs, tongues
with onions, offal trifle, sprinkled
with hundreds-&-thousands
of souls, death-throe

custard. It all looked delicious
& pained us no end. The day we were exiled
the triumphant incumbents
were feasting on our remnants.

Gentrified Times

Men came to the neighbourhood,
their women in tow,

wide-eyed with wealth,
pale-skinned & pregnant

with their soon-to-be kinfolk.
The men tore down the sweetshop

outside which
I once groped my first kiss.

They demolished the flats
where my sweetheart lived.

The park's green blades
where we played

were razed in the furnace
of Progress. The house

where my mother was born
was torn down.

Where am I now? Still
here. Which direction

is what? How
do I divine North

from South, when
the landmarks which bore me

my bearings
are no more? It's only

after the symbols
of your address are demolished,

once the signposts
of your tribe vanish

that you realise their purpose:
those markers

were sacred & placed you
within your location.

Those holy sites
were psychic anchors,

guardians of your dreams.
Stone omens defending

the clan's legacy.
The question now

is this: How
to re-orientate yourself

in a place
you no-longer recognise,

where your sages
lay dead?

PART THREE:

THE CRACK THRU WHICH HE CREPT

"Crack stood for pain & power, chaos & order, the truth behind the lie. Crack was a socio-legal logic grounded in blood."

Dimitri A. Bogazianos

The Story Of Crack

The story of
Crack is
the story
of capital-
ist. A
tract
traceable
back, direct
to descendant
of fiscal
imperative

The story of
Crack is
the story
of al-
chemist. Test-
tube magician
beckons base-
metal meta-
morphosis
from soil
to silver

Dark angels
will
mineral substance
to transmute
form, from
clay
into
gold

The story of
Crack is
the story
of cosmos. Atoms
warmed
in the urn
of lunar
thunder

Nucleus of
vaporous
mass, yearns
thru aeons
of pain
for matter
to happen

A void
the black
shape of
a nebula
hole final-
ly filled
by white
rock
of star
that shines
& is
coveted

The story of
Crack is
the long-
wished answer
to the dilemma:
what would man
do, were he
to hold
a star?

He would
smoke it
& ask for
more

Forever

Something Happened
On The Way To The Crack House

The clock's beak breaks,
the night's creature is present.
I'm led by the heart to a tall block

with stairs that alight to my fate.
I'm not coerced, I seek anaesthetics,
I am an addict. My suitor

is just out of jail. I entrust him
to deliver, a courier of darkness.
Not much further, he says as the stairs bend.

We ascend & I witness the outline
of an instrument tucked in the back of his pants
under a frayed shirt. This is the night when the king

loses his queen, the pack is a joker short
tonight. We soar & the instrument of death
falls from his person - the sound of steel

upon the stone stairwell signals hell.
I look at his face, his intention is plain. I stare
at the blade as it gleams in the half-light

& I know it's intended for my stomach.
The stitch in my soul unwinds its wound
as if to make room for a jewel.

I Am God's Trusted Pharmacist

God gets all the best shit & doesn't need a script. Imagine the size of God's syringe. Now imagine the vein. The stench of His abscess. The infinitude of His abyss. That's some serious shit! You have no idea. Whilst I fill his bag God waits out front of my chemist shop. Seats his godamn ass on a plastic seat. Watches soap operas on the television & laughs his holy ghost off at wooden dialogue, quasi biblical themes of betrayal & salvation. Sets which wobble like a lie nailed to a barn door. God listens to rap music on the radio, says his sons' got rhythm. God says he pop a cap in a mofucking Pontiff. It's Jay-Z's ministry now. God tries on sunglasses, steals lollipops, tuts at the prices of nappies & Paracetamol. He sees the world he cradled wander by the window in pain. God is the great enabler & his step four will floor his AA sponsor. God got emotional scars the size of rivers. In God's case denial *really* is a river in Egypt. Shame is a continent of discontent. God asks me if I've seen Britney Spears lately, says he didn't mean it to turn out the way it did. & the kid from Different Strokes, he says, that shit was fucked up. When I'm done filling his bag, God checks for omissions & says "What, no flavoured condoms?" He thinks I leave the contraception out in the hope of another immaculate conception. I say Jesus Christ, fuck that. It's an accident. We've suffered enough. God, enjoy your drugs!

Anointment

The first chalice of white that anointed my lips,
that ancient thirst lanced at the welt of white heat

was both the first & not the first. In that
the warmth of its presence delivered not shock

of the new, but the choke of remembrance. I had known
this sharp lust, this wild ambush of rushing locus,

this healing balm sentence of peace from all harm
before. All storm dulled in its dulcet caress. Mother

universe, her kiss. Pipe as teat, smoke as clavicle,
umbilical, long-rolling lineage, sure-scrolling

heritage. Song of root, song of extraction.
Familial howl of a son, lost, now recovered by clan.

Made whole again. Crack was recovery of primal memory,
of ancestry. If love is a drug then love was cocaine.

Sing Me A Song

Sing me a song, she says
& lays back all rotund & rag-limbed
upon the frazzled faux-wooden linoleum.

Sing me a song, she says
& kicks her soiled kecks back over her head
as I, amazed, watch them flight
then dead-stop upon a plastic pyre
of long-swigged methadone bottles.

Sing me a song, she says
as her quirky knees un-meet, split
divide across a horizon, left cap to east
right to west. The axis seats
a great hairy beast with herpes.

Sing me a song, she says
& puts two white bone-like fingers
inside her hole's ever-after smile
& squeals, can you see it, is it a girl?

Sing me a song, she says
as I peruse the needle-bruises

track-marks no Indian tracker
with nose to the plains of her terrain
could follow nor fathom in his wisdom.

Sing me a song, she says
as I watch the two knotted scars
like pink coins in the socket of her groin
where she had her veins removed
& wonder what my super power is.

Sing me a song, she says
& I imagine that birth is a cousin
to excretion, babies as faeces.

Sing me a song, she says
& I envisage the drug-addled savage
she is about to emit to my presence.

Sing me a song, she says
& I see it clear as transparent optics:
birth in the shadow of the poor quarter
is the universe emptying its colon.

Sing me a song, she says
as I puke thirteen colours
not a carrot amongst them.

The Prophet

Sometimes, I don't know where the STOP button is. I would like nothing more right now than to fall ill. I don't mean a cold or influenza, nothing domesticated like that. I mean something exotic. Something that undermines the doctor's logic. An illness without an expert or an industry. I want to be the first person to suffer this sickness. I want them to name the disease after me. I would like to be retired to the bed with the immaculate starched white sheets in the room on the ground floor. The glass doors slide open to permit an auburn breeze, a sole tree upon a hill beyond the forecourt. Volunteers tend the grounds. Preserve the garden in its original glory. They tell me that, just before I died, I lifted my hand – oh I was blissfully weak! - & I pointed a pale finger out beyond the green view. They say my final words were, "I have shown you God."

Mother Mercy

If my mother had only known
as I was crowned between her thighs
on the night of my birth
that I would thirst all my life
for truth & congruence.

That I would walk the plains
of the earth beneath a high sun
with fire's reach stitching my hems
as I sought a plain-speaking man.

That I would seek in all I meet
a reciprocation of my dream's end
to no avail. If my mother only knew
the hurt I would reap on my path.

That at the end of my course
my solitary prize would be to unearth
a cache of lies in the rotten mouths
of my peers. That my project
to divine the divinities of existence
for the masses to tie their hopes

to the mast of my sacrament
would lead me to this: her son
sat alone in the world with a knife
at his wrists filling a bowl at his feet
with the river of her red bloodline.

If my mother had only known my fate
she would have closed her legs
at my birth, & forbade my entrance
to the poisoned chalice
of this fallen world.

The Phoenix

There's this grinding feeling of having lost something. It grows around your heart like moss upon a tree. Just look at those green branches clawing after abdicated air. But of course, it was never a tree covered in moss, have you forgotten that as well? It was the house you grew up in, abandoned & moss-struck. Now, where did you put those keys? They say, "Go back inside the room where you had them last." But the room is a shoebox sat atop the wardrobe, containing photographs of imposters wearing masks with your family's faces painted on them. You can't go back now, all the doors are sealed, & time, that sly devil, has cauterised the lanterns. Soon, you'll remember how the phoenix was a fictional fowl created by a shepherd bored of his flock; but you'll forget your own name & your mother's birthday. All that you forget is not lost but awaits you in death. You exit your clothes & enter the water. The wind catches the open window & BANG. You remember everything.

The Lament

This street is a barren plane. Everything
I lean against wanes, all that promises

reneges. So, like all cowards, I get into bed
with the word. I am in cahoots with every

two-bit text in existence. I have backed
the black colt of language. Each sovereign chip

I have is stacked on the dark hieroglyphic.
When night pulls the rope of its window

& the house alight upon the hill is my own
I resort to my bucketful of words. The fire

is not dowsed. Words for the heat on the heath.
Words for the torpor in my heart. I emit

one long note with a reach like a column
of glass, which exits straight up & out from the hole

in the top of my head. This lament
for the alphabet, & all the tongue's orphans.

PART FOUR:

ASPHALT RUNWAYS

"If I can't build a door with this alphabet then it's useless to me."

Miggy Angel

The Bookworm

On a street called road
stands a terrace-shouldered home.
Red door as red as the kin's spilt blood.

Behind this stitch of old brown bricks
sits a flock's nest, decorated not
with twigs, but books.

When the north wind blows
& the windows rattle, & the old man
returns, breathing the fire of his alcohol

the young boy beds down between the pages.

Notes To A Young Mystic

If you should see the grand design
unfurl itself in a realm of light,
& understand how we are angels,
the earth divine, no moment mundane
but infinitely magnificent & worthy of praise,
be careful who you tell.

People covet their poverty of purpose,
their notions of meaninglessness
& their own insignificance.

Go live amongst we street bums, drunks
& pavement shamans. The outcast understands
how the saints & sons of comets
must walk the margins of this comatose province.

I Am The Riot You Seek

For those who crossed distances
to witness civil disobedience

I am the riot you seek

I am the seed wrought hot
in the soil of this moment

I am the riot you seek

I am the root & the branch
The great height, the great tree

Just me, I am the riot you seek

I was not born to an epoch
I am tied to no instant, no idol, nor script

I am the riot you seek

I am an exchange of energies
The bedrock of galaxies

The change which is endless

I am the riot you seek

Spirit barks its dissent
thru the halls of my marrow

I am the riot you seek

Nucleus of an atomic furnace
sets torch to my speech

I am the riot you seek

Light from the farthest star
sparks the engine of my motion

I am the riot you seek

I have railed for aeons
against the dynamos of heaven
to render void form

I am the riot you seek

I am the principle particle
who rides the black night of history
for all eternity

I am the riot you seek

I am the object without subject
The subject without object

I am the riot you seek

I am the space
where the whole world takes place

I am the riot you seek

I am the presence
whose existence
is resistance

I am the riot you seek

Yes, it is I

whose evolutionary path
is a revolutionary act

I am the riot you seek

Let your life be the chrysalis
for the great metamorphosis

Yes you are the riot you seek

Songs Sung In The First Register

Songs sung in the first register will reach your bones before they tempt your ears

Songs sung in the first register will make it into the hearts of beasts before they reach the chests of businessmen or dignitaries

Songs sung in the first register are boiled long in the song's cauldron

Ferment thru centuries in the skeleton's collective memory

Songs sung in the first register scold the lips of master craftsmen who attempt to adopt them, but are as kisses upon the lips of the amateurish attempt

Songs sung in the first register anoint the layman & curse the expert

Songs sung in the first register will be heard thru space

Songs sung in the first register will be known as the theme to death which is sung to celebrate life

Songs sung in the first register will never be written in ink

But shall be composed upon the lung & if ink then blood alone

Songs sung in the first register will never choose a preference for one element

Shall be as one with earth, wind, fire, & water

The ocean of furnace, the fire's sea, the molten urn's coldest kernel

Songs sung in the first register will circumvent practice, eject thought's premise

Will require no art, no critic, critique nor tradition

Songs sung in the first register will be the death of models

Will be the death of the familial, the societal, the umbilical's unspooling, the post-coital post-colonial post-chronicle post-document pre-language song

Songs sung in the first register will accompany your birth, orchestrate the dirge of your betrayal, partner your demise, lead the convoy of your creation in abominable ruin: your one signature song

Songs sung in the first register will not make the radio play-lists of your epoch tho shall be evident by their absence

Songs sung in the first register will be eternally mercurial, perennially elusive, will never be tied to trend nor shackled to favour nor fashion, will be immune to recording devices, escape photography, averse to paper, resistant to stages created to capture them

Songs sung in the first register will be a covenant kept in the marrow's keep, guarded by the black crow of your hurt, who is, as we speak, about to sing

Narrow Alleys

Detectives under cover of civilian attire
sat in an inauspicious drive
eating sandwiches of stolen horseradish
& other captured souls, whilst
sipping cups of lukewarm brainwaves
from a far off century, plot in their jalopy
& watch my home. They
monitor my movements.

Tactics culled from Seventies' cop shows,
stake-outs at full moon & low tide for high stakes.
I walk down to the end of my road
stand at my corner & wave.

They tell me where I've been & what I've done,
who I've seen & who's been & gone.
These men & their procedurals
wanna reduce me to my externals:
my habits & movements.

They seek to invalidate my internals:
my oceans & immensities.

I am pursued thru narrow alleys
by Reductionists.

Today, did you see
my stomach turn foodstuff to excrement?
My mind filter the ephemeral
thru prime urban Sanskrit material?

In my palm I stir base metals
& earth minerals
return them to gold petals.

This is no mystery, just plain forgotten
human alchemy: Poetry.
My every heartbeat
accompanies the universal symphony.
I wear the perennial dust
of the centuries
in my underarm hair
but I am pursued thru narrow alleys
by Reductionists.

The Linguist

As I am writing these words you are reading them. But our memories are poor, & I forget what it is I'm supposed to be writing - & you forget each word as soon as you read it. As we go deeper into this ritual the words act to further purge us of our memories. Until we cannot remember what each word means or has ever meant. Words which once were portals thru which we were transported have lost their ability to traffic. Words like: cobweb, window, birthright, thunder. See? Nothing. We stare at these empty black etchings & watch as a large red rose replete with thorns emerges from the page. Whilst you run to fetch a pale of water for our new Eden I continue writing, as the rose is my favourite sentinel, & I am its trusted disciple.

The Bell

I wish to give to you
a bell.

This is a bell.

You see it, don't you?
It is the shape
of a policeman's helmet
but not as comical.

This bell
was forged in the mouth
of the universe.

It glistens like a filling.

When you look into it
you see your reflection.

Smile at yourself.

Knock a knuckle on it.

Listen: the bell rings
like a siren
in an ocean of mystery.

When the philosopher says
he cannot decipher
the bell

When the archaeologist says
he cannot discover
the bell

When the mortician says
he cannot embalm
the bell

When the doctor says
he cannot diagnose
the bell

When the scientist says
he cannot see, measure
or weigh
the bell

That the bell is not evident
that therefore
the bell
does not exist

Take yourself off
to the yellow fields
beyond the city walls.

Ring your bell
as loud as you can
& laugh like a child.

I wish to give to you
a bell.

This is a bell.

Please, cherish
the little bell.
Now, it's yours.

Scallywag Standing On The Balcony Of Tate Modern

There are so many tourists inside the Tate Modern & they've all just come from fucking each other in the lifts whilst you were taking the stairs. So you're resentful & they bump into you with their elbows, with their supreme genes & pristine liberal educations. I mean they will literally smack you full in the face with two thousand years of belligerent European arrogance & if you query them tersely on their conduct they will hold their arms up, wave their hands & smile, "No no no," inoculated against accusation or inquiry. However, alone in this coming-together of coded architecture & self-satisfaction walks an artist. A star-blessed individual, ink-scarred & born under a curious hex, who alone has apprehended the ramifications of the tragedy of Art history, has imbibed every monstrous thought & mutinous feint or sleight of the apparatus, held it all within his axis, insulated it like a chrysalis. You stand on the balcony of the Tate Modern holding the incandescent crystal born of your will to self-realisation. It is night, there is a perpendicular breeze. You stare out at the city & light a cigarette with the whole of Art practice & theory at your back. Tonight, London is ablaze, like your wild mind, with neon.

♦ fin ♦

Acknowledgements

Just like our old friend Prometheus & his mythological antics, a book is an attempt to steal fire from the gods. I would like to thank my co-defendants in this criminal endeavour, persons without whom this book would not exist & the gods would not be short a humble lantern this fine, mysterious evening.

I would like to thank my wonderful family, my daughter, Rosa, mother, Sheila, & sister, Lucy. Thanks to you all for putting up with my trying tempos & loving me enough to be a creative person.

& my mrs, the playwright Emteaz Hussain - I recall the day I entered your northern home with its extensive bookshelf library as a defining moment. The key to the magical kingdom was passed to a scallywag, right there. Thank you for everything.

Thanks to the workers at every institution or agency I've ever passed thru. Especially tho, much love & gratitude to Peter Kane, once of City Road crisis intervention unit.

Thanks to all my colleagues at Double Impact & the writers who attend the weekly creative writing workshop I facilitate there. Keep writing, guys. You are an inspiration.

Thanks to the rooms & everyone in them, keeping alive the tradition of the campfire, the oral tradition, stories passed from the heart to the tongue to the ear & back to the heart. It's how we heal, you know.

Thanks to everyone who was in or around the Royal court young peoples' theatre back in 97-98. Especially Steve Gilroy, Carl Miller, Aoife Mannix, Ola Animashuwan, Roy Williams & Jess Walters. You guys told me I was an artist before I knew what one was.

Thanks to my first reader & trusted manuscript consultant, Julie Pearn.

Thanks to my creative partner in crime, the music man John Freer.

Thanks to the photographer, Trish Evans, for allowing me to use your wonderful photography for the front cover of this book.

Thanks to everyone who has ever encouraged my creativity, in whichever way, large or small, and to all the amazing writers & supporters who took the time to provide endorsements for the book.

Of course, numerous thanks go to Mac of Celandor, & Glen Jarvis of Climbing Mountains. I think we did something proper special, fellas. Thanks for the opportunity to create this book & I salute your astuteness in spotting great work when you see it (if I say so meself!).

Finally, thanks to everyone who has parted with some hard-earned in order to own a copy of this, my first book of poems.

A Special Thanks From The Publishers

Miggy Angel is an exceptional poet & wordsmith & this, his first published work, provides us with a powerful, gritty & vital snapshot of urban life in contemporary Britain.

But producing this book provided us, the publishers, with a problem: the need to find a cover image powerful enough to fit the words within. Nottingham's dynamic cultural & artistic community provided a timely solution – a visit to an exhibition of the work of artist & photographer Trish Evans.

Our extraordinary cover image is taken from Trish's collection of vibrant & astonishing photographs that capture the freedom, vitality & energy of free-running in abandoned, forgotten & often hidden spaces. We are tremendous admirers of her work & thrilled she allowed us to use it. Thank you Trish!

To learn more about Trish Evans & her beautiful & inspiring work please visit her website,
www.road-work.org.uk.